SCHIRMER'S LIBRARY
OF MUSICAL CLASSICS

Vol. 148

CARL CZERNY

Op. 636

Preliminary School
of Finger Dexterity

For the Piano

Edited, Revised, and Fingered by
GIUSEPPE BUONAMICI

✛

G. SCHIRMER, Inc.

DISTRIBUTED BY
HAL•LEONARD®
CORPORATION
7777 W. BLUEMOUND RD. P.O. BOX 13819 MILWAUKEE, WI 53213

Die Vorschule zur Fingerfertigkeit.

(Preliminary School of Finger Dexterity.)

24 Progressive Studies.

Book I.

Allegro. (♩ = 84.)

C. CZERNY. Op.636.

1.✛)

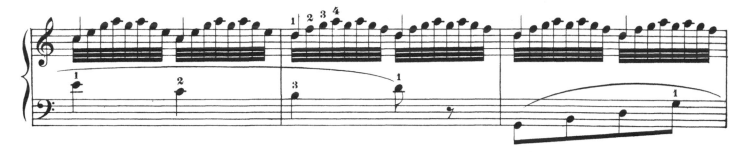

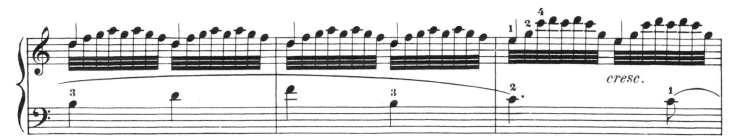

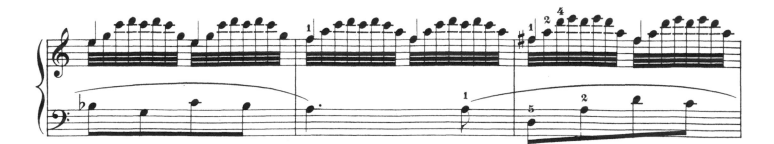

✛) It is excellent practice to transpose this study both a semitone lower and a semitone higher, using the same fingering.

Printed in the U.S.A.

4

Allegro. (♩ = 76.)

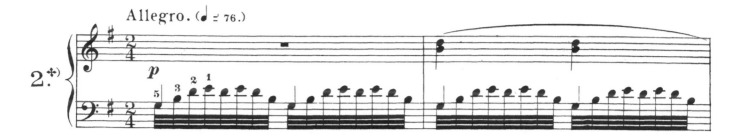

2.✦)

p

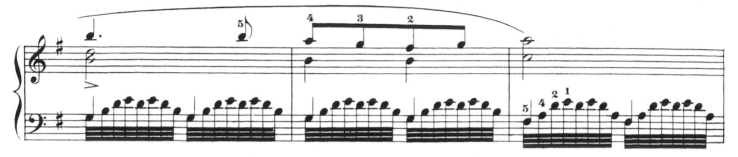

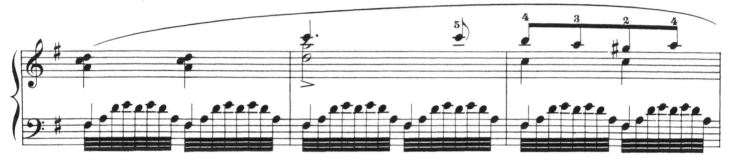

cresc.

f dim.

p

✦) Also practice transposed into G♭.

11154

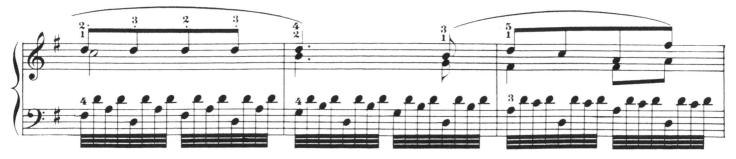

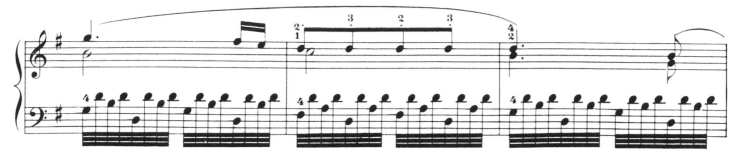

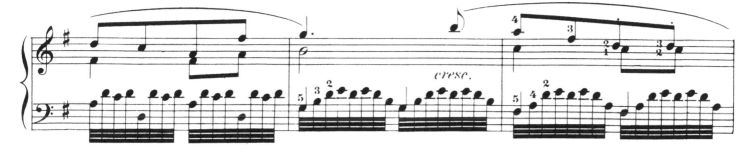

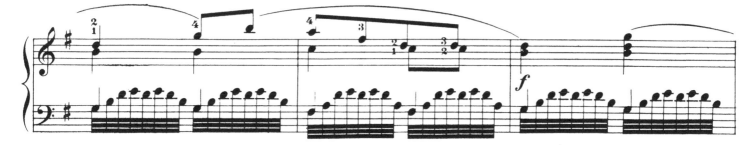

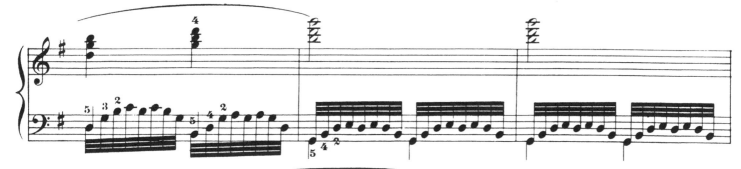

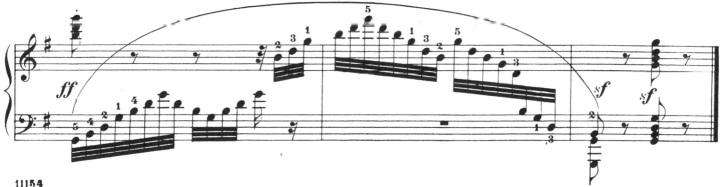

Allegro vivace. ($\quad$ = 144.)

3.

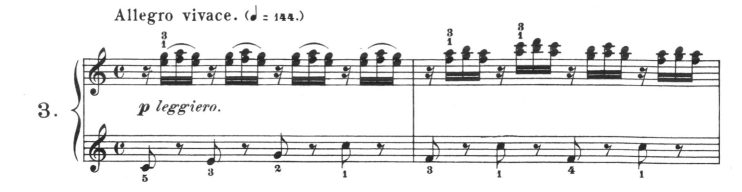

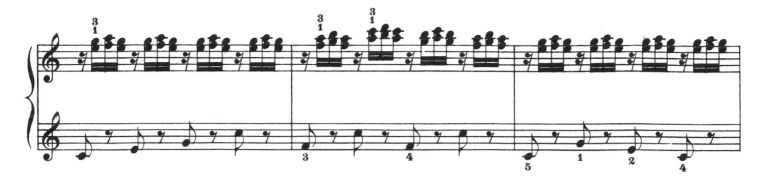

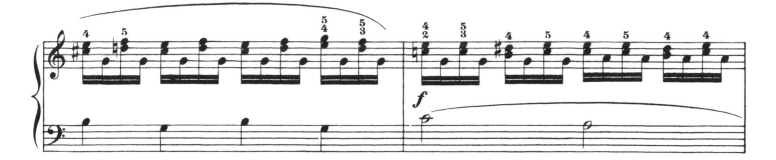

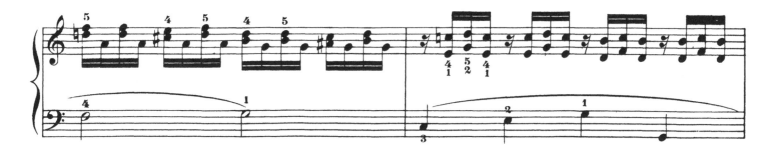

8

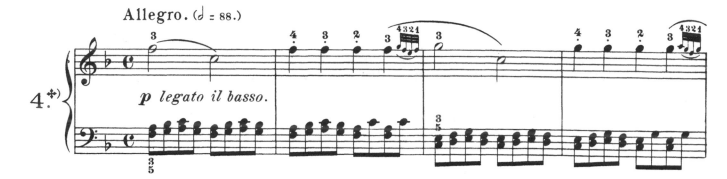

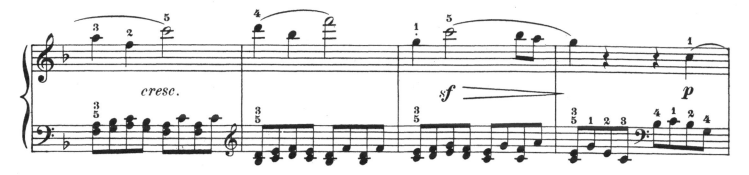

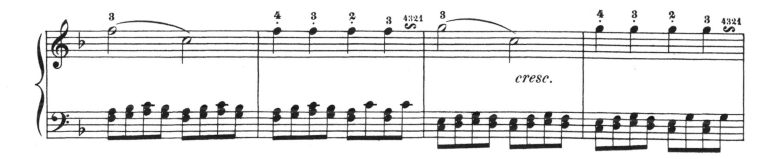

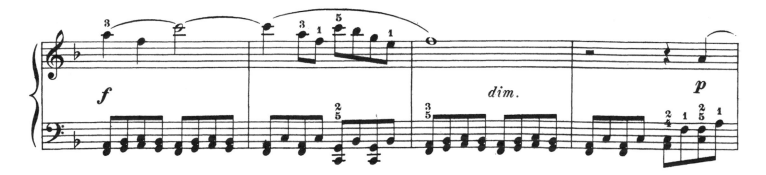

✤) It is also excellent practice to transpose this study into F♯, in which case the necessary changes may be made in the right-hand fingering, that for the left remaining unchanged.

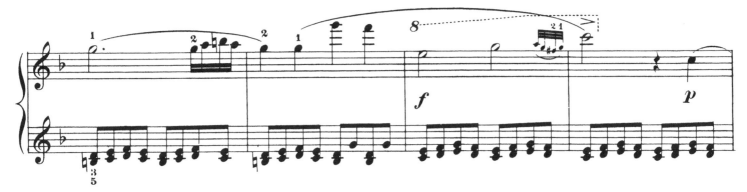

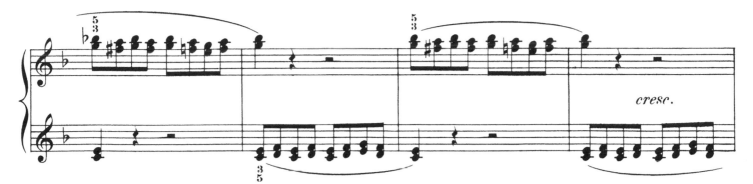

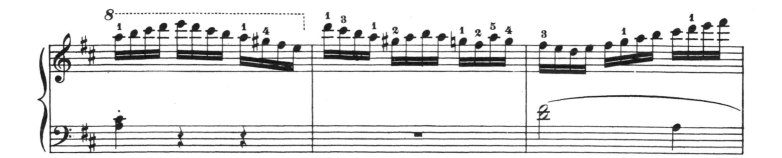

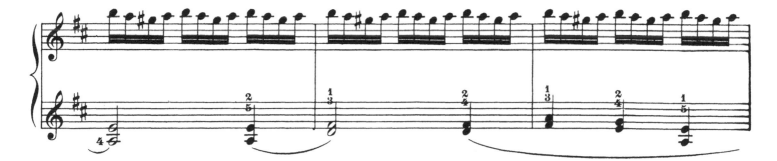

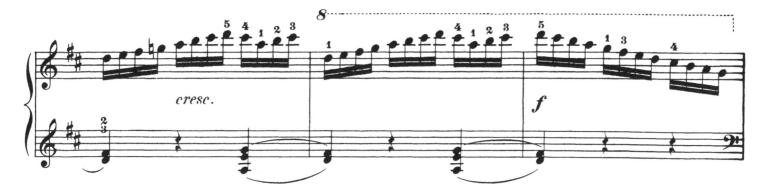

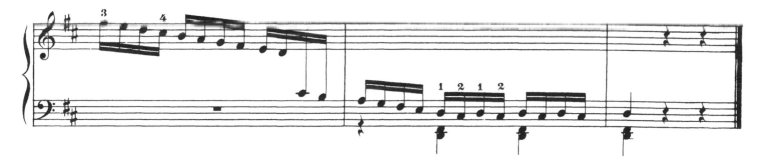

Allegro. ($\bullet = 160$.)

6.

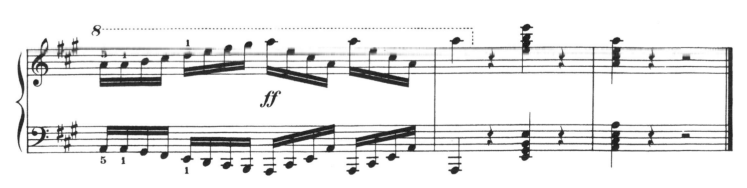

Allegro moderato. ($\quad$ = 108.)

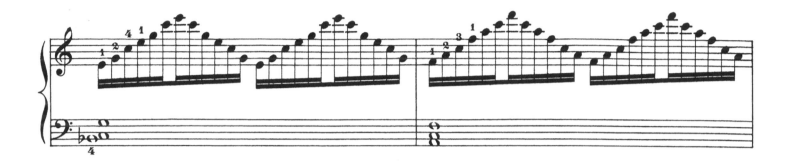

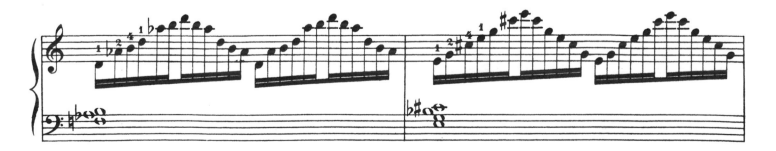

✦) Also transpose into C♯ and C♭, in either case changing the fingering of the 16th measure.

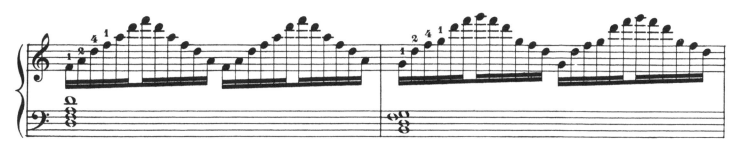

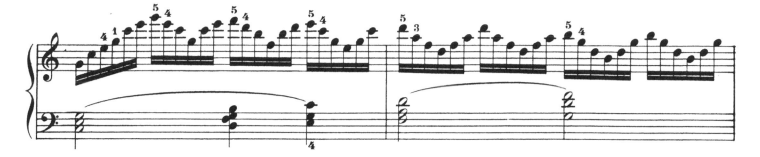

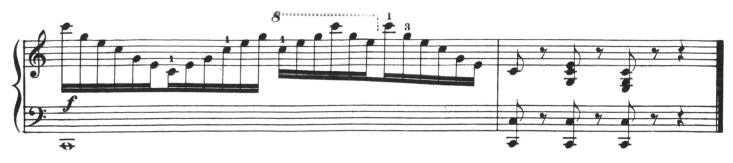

Allegro moderato. ($\bullet$ = 144.)

8.*)

*) Transpose like the preceding study.

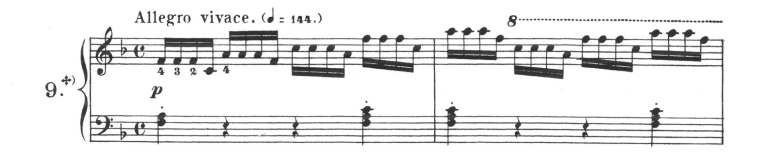

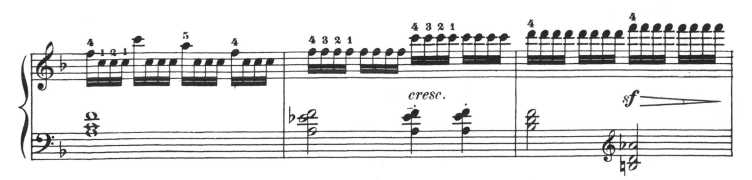

✥) Transpose into F♯, and adhere to the given fingering, though it present difficulties in measures 3 and 4.

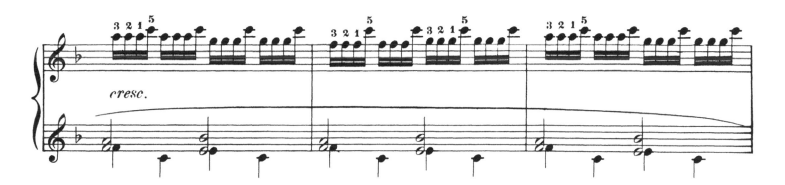

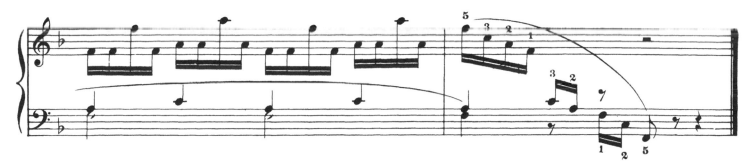

Die Vorschule zur Fingerfertigkeit.

(Preliminary School of Finger-Dexterity.)

24 Progressive Studies.

Book II.

C. CZERNY. Op. 636.

Allegro. (♩ = 160.)

10.⁺)

⁺) Also practise in B-major, with the same fingering.

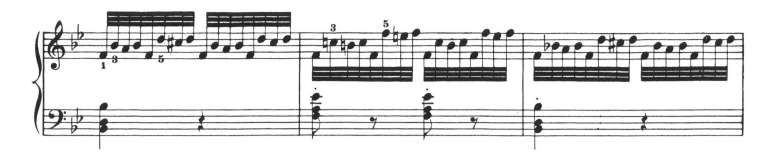

Allegro commodo. ($\quad$ = 132.)

11.

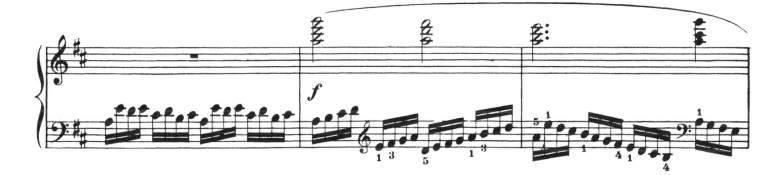

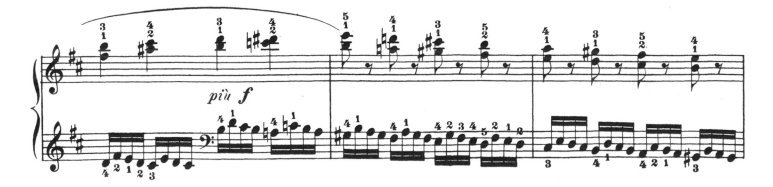

Allegro leggiero. (♩=176.)

12.

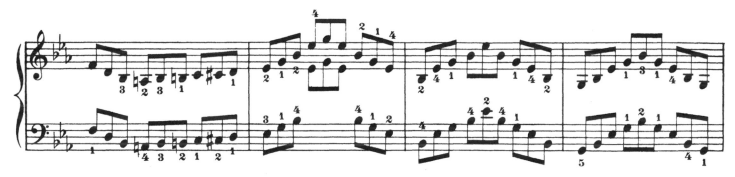

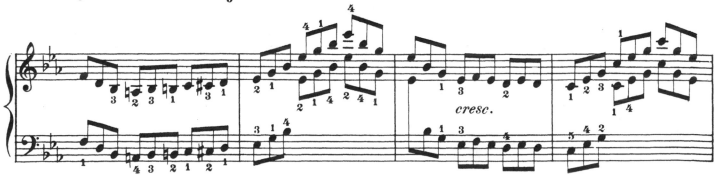

13.

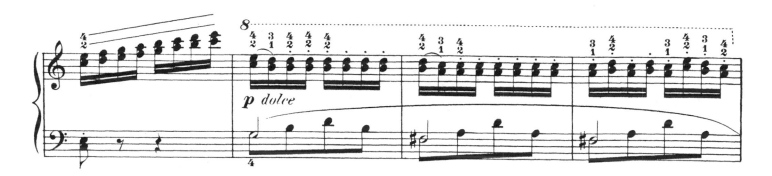

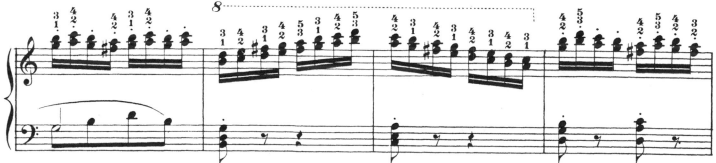

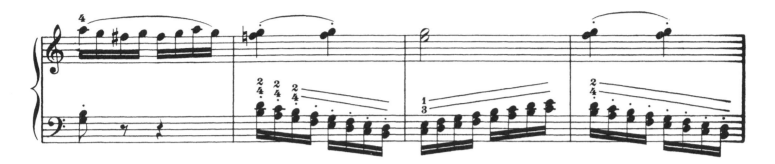

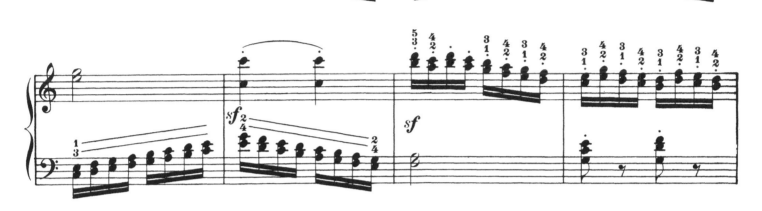

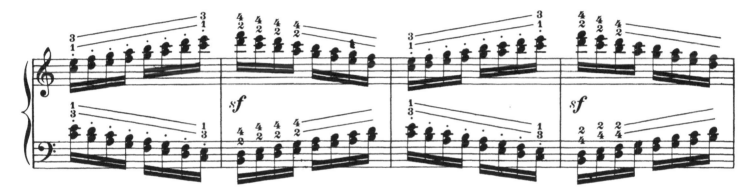

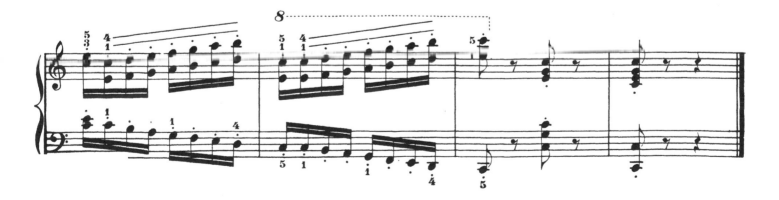

Allegro vivace. (♩.= 88.)

14.

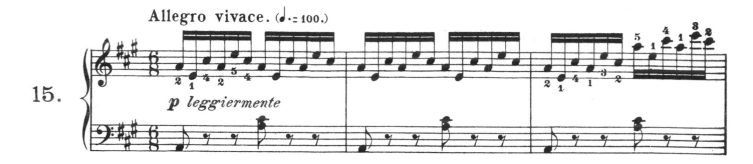

15.

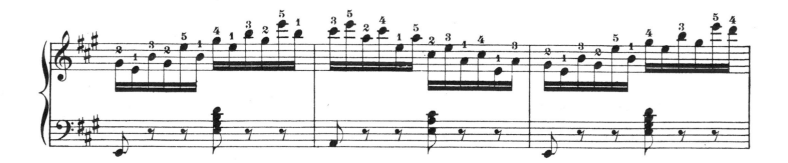

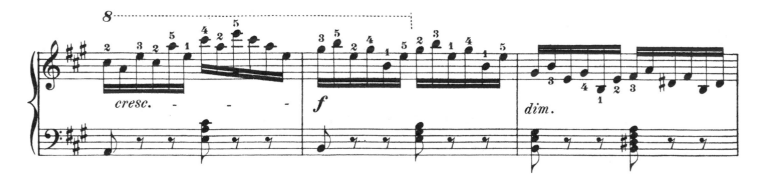

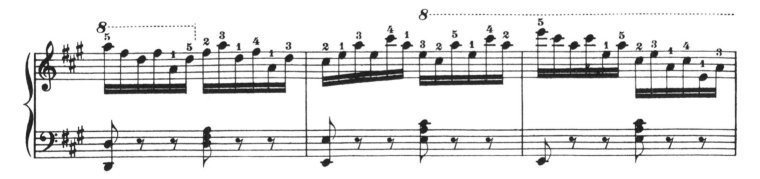

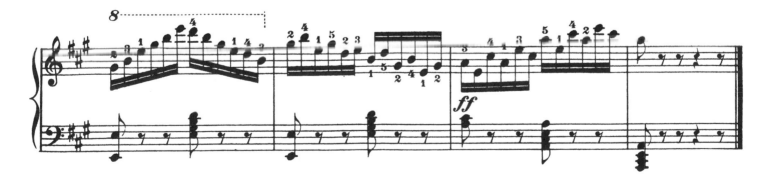

Allegro moderato. (♩ = 132.)

16.⁺)

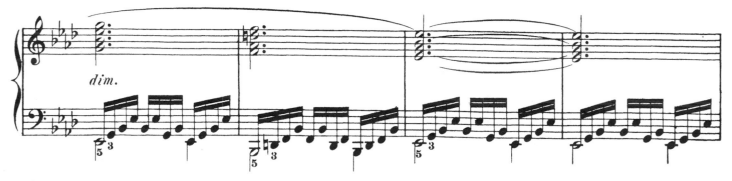

⁺) Also transpose into A-major.

Die Vorschule zur Fingerfertigkeit.

(Preliminary School of Finger-Dexterity.)

24 Progressive Studies.

Book III.

Allegro vivo e scherzoso. (♩ = 132.)

C. CZERNY. Op. 636.

17.

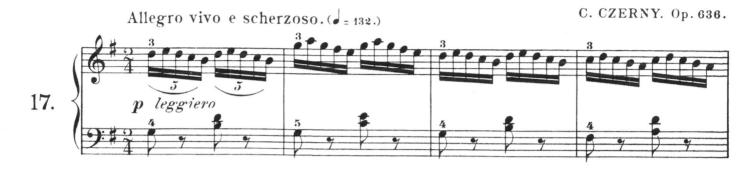

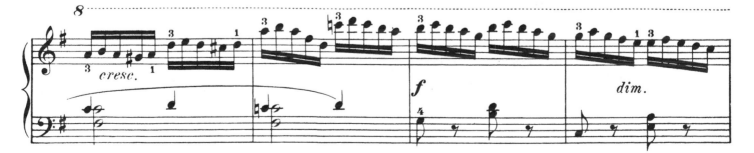

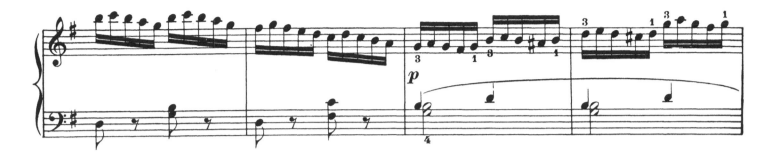

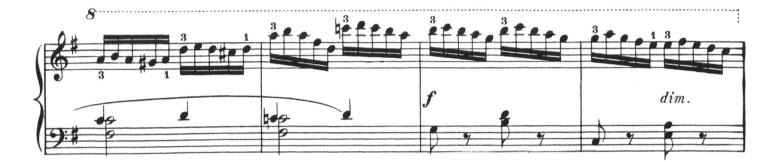

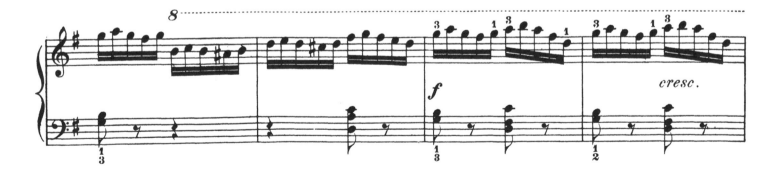

Moderato. ($\flat$ = 138.)

18.

p sempre legato

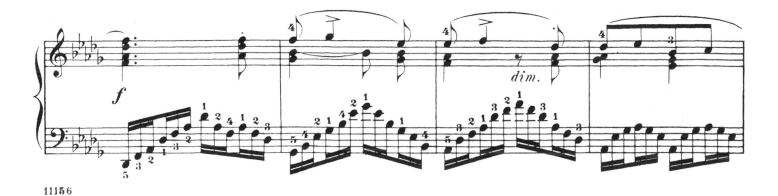

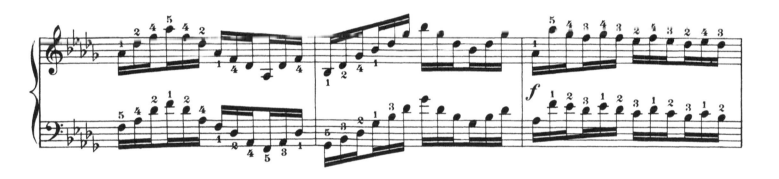

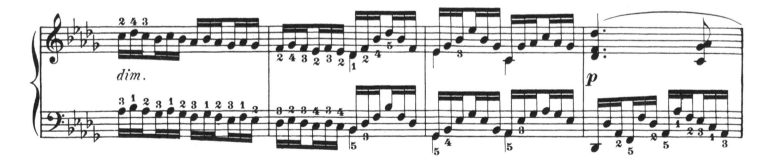

19.

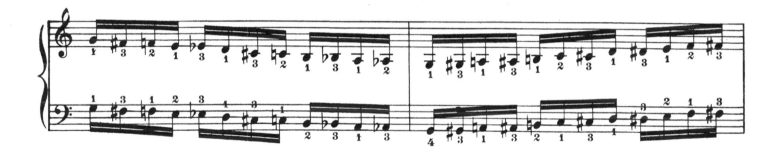

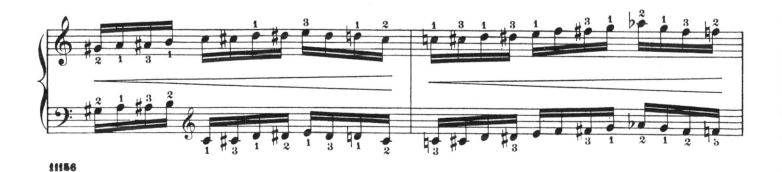

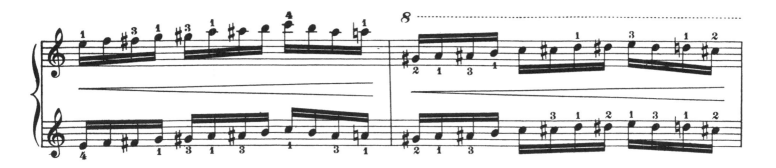

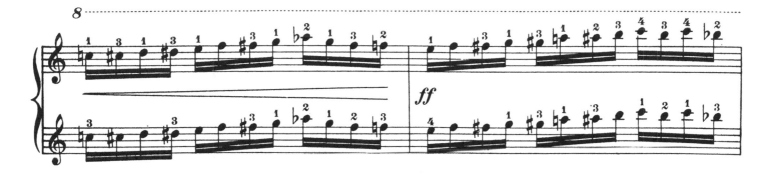

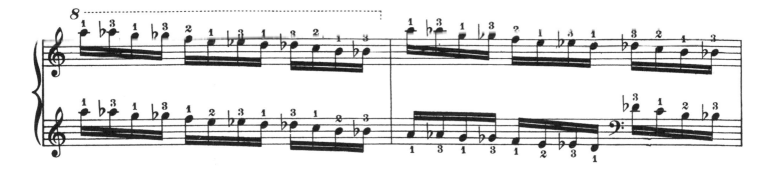

Allegro veloce. ($\bullet$ = 104.)

20.

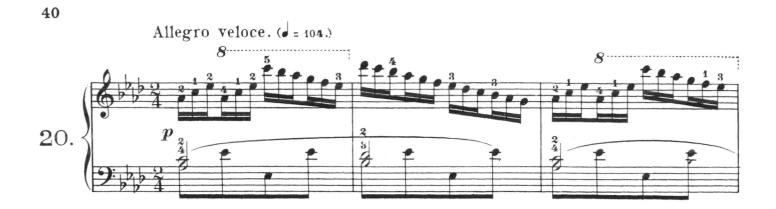

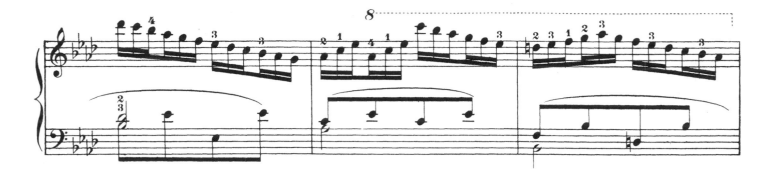

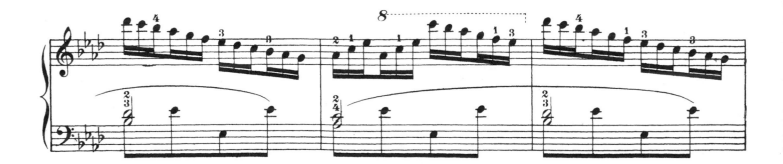

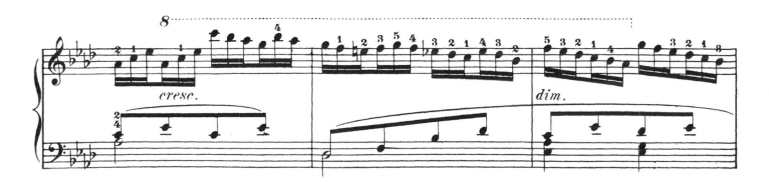

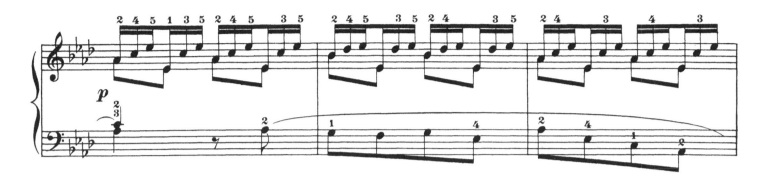

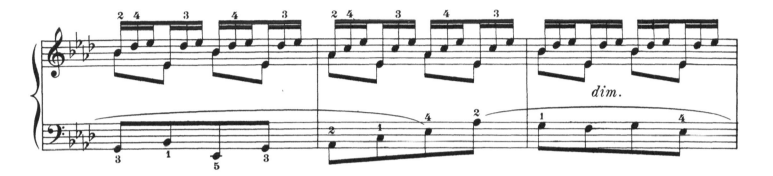

Allegro vivo. ($\bullet$ = 112.)

21.

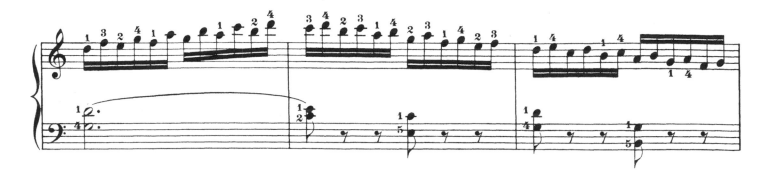

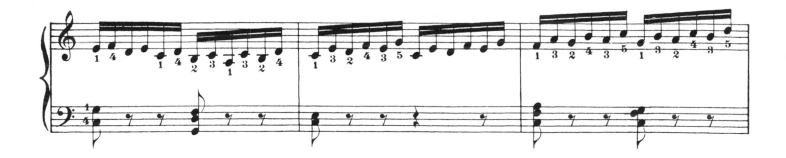

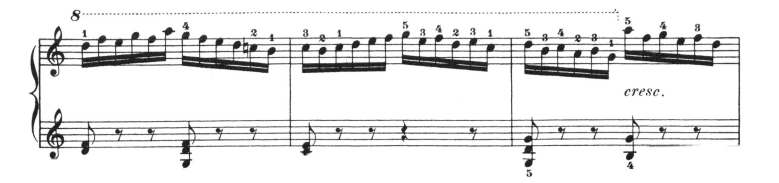

Allegro comodo. (♩ = 100.)

22.⁑)

⁑) Also transpose into F♯.

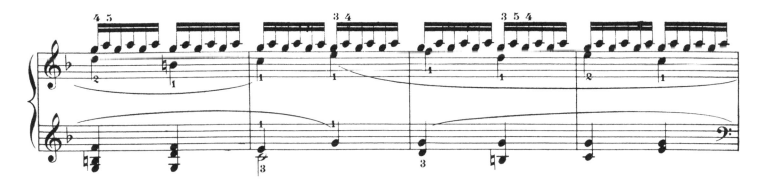

Molto Allegro. (♩ = 160.)

23.

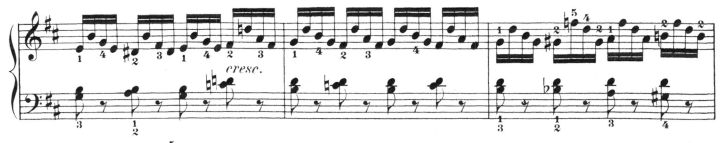

24.

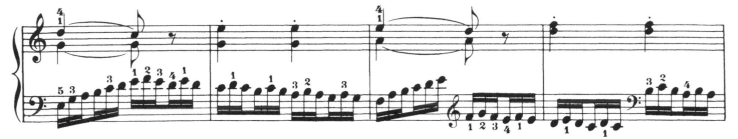

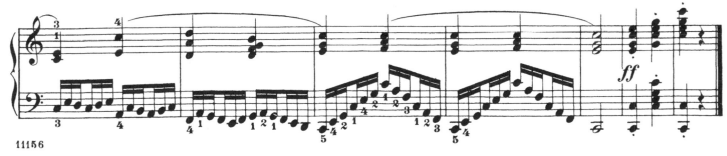